BY CARLOS FUENTES

ILLUSTRATED BY K.E. LEWIS

Target Skill Main Idea

Where will Sam and Cass go?

Sam and Cass have big bags.

They must look for a cab.

2

Can we catch a cab?

What time is it, Sam?

I will look, Cass.

Will a cab come?

Where is a cab?

Check the time, Sam!

I will check, Cass.

It takes too long to get a cab.

Check the time, Sam!

I will check, Cass.

We can get a bus.

Which bus do we take?

There is the bus stop.

We can not miss the bus.

Sam spots the bus. Cass waves to it.

Sam and Cass will zip off.

Just in time!

Is it time to munch lunch?

Check the time, Sam!

I do not need to check, Cass!